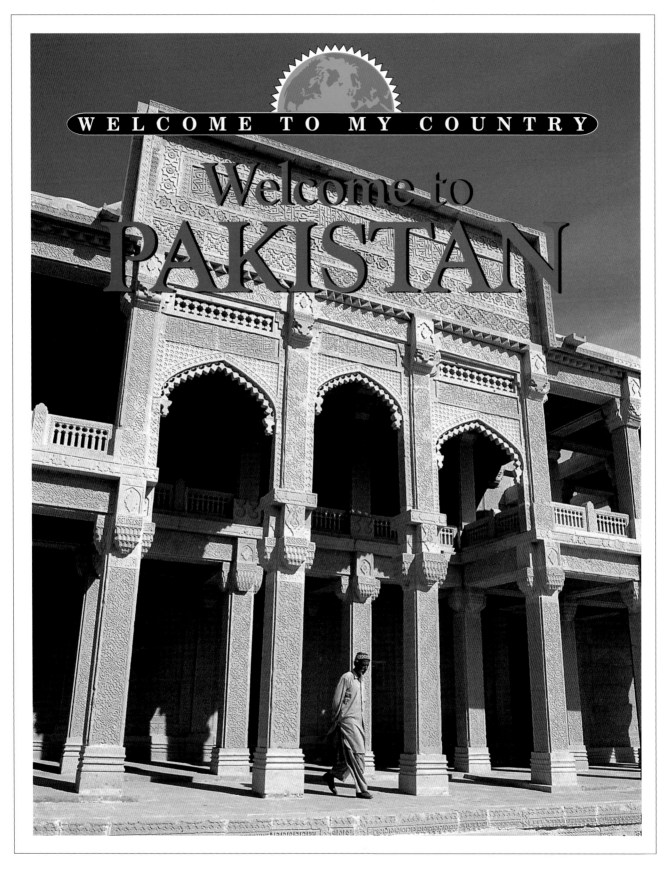

Welcome to PAKISTAN

W

FRANKLIN WATTS
LONDON•SYDNEY

501281902

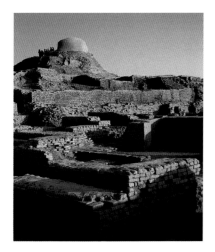

This edition first published in 2005 by
Franklin Watts
96 Leonard Street
London EC2A 4XD

Franklin Watts Australia
45-51 Huntley Street
Alexandria NSW 2015

This edition is published for sale only in the United Kingdom & Eire.

© Marshall Cavendish International (Asia) Pte Ltd 2005
Originated and designed by Times Editions–Marshall Cavendish
an imprint of Marshall Cavendish International (Asia) Pte Ltd
A member of the Times Publishing Group
Times Centre, 1 New Industrial Road
Singapore 536196

Written by: Karen Kwek & Jameel Haque
Editor: Melvin Neo
Designer: Geoslyn Lim
Picture researcher: Susan Jane Manuel

A CIP catalogue record for this book
is available from the British Library.

ISBN 0 7496 6018 X

All rights reserved. No part of this publication may be reproduced
or transmitted in any form or by any means, or stored in any
retrieval system of any nature without the prior written permission
of Marshall Cavendish International (Asia) Pte Ltd.

Printed in Singapore

PICTURE CREDITS
Art Directors & TRIP Photographic Library:
    6, 11, 27, 28, 32, 34 (bottom), 35, 43
Camera Press: 12, 17
Downtown MoneyPoint: 44 (both)
Getty Images/Hulton Archive: 13, 14, 16, 39
The Hutchison Library: cover, 3 (centre), 5, 20
John R. Jones: 45
Lonely Planet Images: 8, 26
NewsPix: 36
Christine Osborne Pictures: 2, 10, 19,
    34 (top), 38
Pakistan High Commission, Singapore: 15 (top)
Pakistan National Council of the Arts: 30 (both),
    31 (top)
Topham Picturepoint: 3 (top), 7, 9 (both),
    15 (centre), 15 (bottom), 18, 21, 23, 25,
    29, 37, 40, 41
Nik Wheeler: 1, 3 (bottom), 4, 22,
    31 (bottom), 33
Alison Wright: 24

Digital Scanning by Superskill Graphics Pte Ltd

Contents

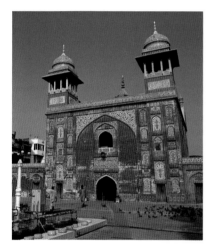

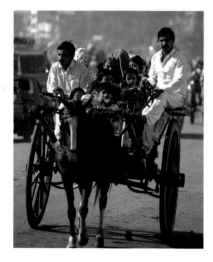

Words that appear in the glossary are printed in **boldface** type the first time they occur in the text.

Welcome to Pakistan!

Pakistan is a young country in South Asia. It was once part of India, ruled by the British, but in 1947 it became a separate nation. The country's official name is Islamic Republic of Pakistan. Although its population includes many **ethnic** groups, almost all of the people are Muslims. Let's explore beautiful Pakistan and meet its **diverse** people!

Opposite: Markets on the streets of Pakistan's big cities sell food and craft items. This market is in Peshawar.

Below: The Prime Minister's Secretariat Building is a magnificent government office structure in the city of Islamabad, the capital of Pakistan.

The Flag of Pakistan

Pakistan's flag is green with a vertical white stripe down the left side. Green stands for the country's Muslims. White represents people of other faiths. The **crescent** and five-pointed star are traditional symbols of the Islamic religion.

The Land

Pakistan's southern boundary is on the Arabian Sea. Moving clockwise from the southwest to the southeast, Pakistan is surrounded by the countries of Iran, Afghanistan, China and India.

In an area of about 803,940 square kilometres, Pakistan has mountain ranges, flatlands and deserts. K2 in the Karakoram Range is the country's highest mountain. K2 rises to a height of 8,611 metres.

Below:
Stretching across northern Pakistan, the Karakoram Range forms one of the world's highest mountain ranges. In fact, K2 is also the world's second-highest mountain.

Left:
Many rivers in Pakistan, including the Indus River, start in the Hindu Kush Range along the country's northwestern boundary. The Himalayas also stretch across northern Pakistan.

In central and southeastern Pakistan, the Indus River, which is the country's main waterway, crosses an area of flat, **fertile** land known as the Indus Plain. This plain is an important agricultural area, especially in the northernmost province of Punjab.

At the southern end of the plain, the province of Sindh has fertile land along the Indus River, but the rest of the land is very dry. The rugged landscape of the southwestern Balochistan **Plateau** is also very dry. Few people live there.

Climate

In northern Pakistan, summers are mild, but winters are cold, with temperatures often below freezing. Southern areas are warmer. Summer temperatures in the Indus Plain, range from 32° to 49° Celsius, falling to about 13° C in winter.

Areas along the Arabian Sea have a **humid** climate. Otherwise, Pakistan is very dry and gets little rainfall. The northern areas receive the most rain.

Above: During spring in north-western Pakistan, the mountain tops are still covered with snow when the apricot trees start to bloom.

Plants and Animals

A variety of trees grow in Pakistan. Areas close to the sea have mangrove forests. The drier southern regions have mulberry trees and date palms. Oak, spruce and pine trees grow in northern forests. Only small **alpine** plants can survive high in the mountains.

The mountains are also home to bears and leopards, while jackals, wild cats and foxes are found throughout the country. Pakistan's birds include eagles, falcons, wood ducks and geese.

Above:
The snow leopard is an endangered animal that lives in the mountains of northern Pakistan. This shy, majestic animal is not often seen because its fur blends in with its surroundings.

Left: The Siberian ibex is a type of wild goat with huge horns. It lives in the mountains of northern Pakistan.

History

People have been living in what is now Pakistan for over eight thousand years. The Indus Valley **civilisation**, which is considered one of the world's first great civilisations, lived there over four thousand years ago and **flourished** for about a thousand years. Then, **Aryans** moved in from Central Asia, bringing a form of the Hindu religion with them. Between 500 B.C. and A.D. 700, many empires and kingdoms ruled the area.

Below:
The ancient city of Mohenjo-Daro was one of many well-planned cities built by the Indus Valley civilisation.

Left: This painting shows Emperor Akbar the Great passing the Mughal crown to his son, Prince Salim, who was later known as Jahangir.

Islam and the Mughal Empire

Arab Muslims brought Islam to Sindh in the seventh and eighth centuries. From 1206 until the end of the Mughal Empire, Muslim rulers controlled most of India, including the land that is now Pakistan. The Mughal Empire was one of the most famous of India's Muslim kingdoms. From 1526 until the early eighteenth century, its strong leaders continually expanded Mughal territory. Mughal rulers promoted literature, art, architecture and music and, although Muslim, encouraged religious freedom.

British Rule

As the Mughal Empire weakened, the British, who had been trading in India since the 1600s, gained power. In 1858, they took over many Indian territories, which became known as British India.

Britain made many improvements to British India, including introducing the British education system. By the early 1900s however, Indians wanted a stronger voice in government, and Muslims wanted a separate country.

Above: In 1947, Muslim leader Ali Jinnah (*third from right*) met with British and Hindu leaders to discuss dividing British India by religions. When the Hindus and Muslims could not agree on the division, the Indian Independence Act of 1947 created a separate Muslim nation called Pakistan.

Independence

On 14 August 1947, Pakistan became an independent country divided into East Pakistan and West Pakistan. As the new nation struggled with unstable leadership and a poor economy, East Pakistan became increasingly unhappy with West Pakistan and wanted more power in government. In 1971, India invaded East Pakistan, starting a war with Pakistan. When India won the war, East Pakistan became a separate country called Bangladesh.

Below: By 1971, the unrest between East and West Pakistan had started a civil war. **Sikh** soldiers from East Pakistan fought for freedom from West Pakistan. On 16 December 1971, East Pakistan became Bangladesh.

A Troubled Country

The break-up of Pakistan did not bring peace. In 1977, Zulfikar Ali Bhutto, who had been the president of West Pakistan, was forced out of office by army general Mohammad Zia ul-Haq. After Zia died in 1988, Zulfikar's daughter, Benazir Bhutto, became prime minister. When she was forced out of power in 1990, Nawaz Sharif was elected prime minister. Bhutto regained control in 1993. Sharif was reelected in 1997. In October 1999, Pakistan's leadership changed again, following a **coup** led by General Pervez Musharraf.

Left: This soldier is standing guard outside the Punjab Assembly building in Lahore. When General Musharraf took control over the government of Pakistan in 1999, he established military rule for the fourth time since the country became independent.

Liaquat Ali Khan (1895–1951)

In 1923, Liaquat Ali Khan joined Mohammad Ali Jinnah in the fight for Pakistan's independence. In 1947, he became the new nation's first prime minister.

Liaquat Ali Khan

Benazir Bhutto (1953–)

Named Pakistan's prime minister in 1988, Benazir Bhutto became the first woman to lead an Islamic country. In 1990, she was accused of **corruption** and was forced out of power. She returned to office in 1993 but was forced out again in 1996.

Benazir Bhutto

Imran Ahmed Khan Niazi (1952–)

Considered one of Pakistan's best cricket players, Imran Ahmed Khan Niazi led the country's national team to victory in the 1991–1992 World Cup competition. He retired from cricket in 1992 and entered politics.

Imran Ahmed Khan Niazi

Government and the Economy

Since Musharraf took over, Pakistan's government has changed. The country used to be a **federal republic** led by a president and a prime minister. A **parliament** elected both government leaders and made the country's laws.

After the 1999 coup, Musharraf formed the National Security Council which is now Pakistan's most powerful governing body. In 2001, Musharraf appointed himself president.

Left: Before taking over as Pakistan's top government leader, General Pervez Musharraf was Chief of Army Staff and head of the Joint Chiefs of Staff. Although he is now Pakistan's head of state, he remains head of the army too.

Left: This building in Islamabad is the home of the Supreme Court which is Pakistan's highest court. Another federal court, called the Shari'a Court, tries cases according to Islamic Law. Provinces have high courts as well as district and village courts.

Provinces and Local Governments

Pakistan is made up of four provinces: Balochistan, Sindh, Punjab and North-West Frontier. Each of these provinces is run by a governor, who reports to a chief minister. The government of each province is broken down into divisions, and each division into districts.

Besides its four provinces, Pakistan also has eleven Federally Administered Tribal Areas and the Islamabad Capital Territory. The local governments for these areas report directly to Pakistan's president, General Musharraf.

A Struggling Economy

Since becoming an independent nation, Pakistan has struggled to improve its economy. Problems such as an unstable government, a fast-growing population and increasing debt to other countries have made Pakistan poor.

Almost half of Pakistan's workforce is involved in agriculture. Most of the country's farms are in Punjab, which has flat land and a good water supply.

Above: The Arabian Sea, off Pakistan's southern coast, provides a variety of fish, including salmon, mackerel and shrimp. These fishermen are unloading a day's catch at Karachi's fishing harbour.

Industry and Resources

Less than 20 per cent of Pakistan's workforce have manufacturing jobs. The most important manufacturing industry is cotton fabrics or textiles. Other industries produce paper, food products and construction materials.

Coal mining is one of Pakistan's oldest industries but the quality of the coal is very poor. The country's other natural resources include petroleum, natural gas, copper and iron ore.

Left: These workers in Sindh province are **threshing** rice. Because most of Pakistan's farms do not have modern machinery, workers must use traditional farming methods.

People and Lifestyle

The people of Pakistan belong to many ethnic groups. Each group has its own culture, language and traditions. The five main groups are Punjabis, Sindhis, Pashtuns, Baloch and *muhajirs*.

Pakistan's largest ethnic group, the Punjabis, make up about two-thirds of the population. Because Punjabis live in the fertile Punjab province, most of them have agricultural jobs.

Below: These girls are from an Islamic school in Sindh province. Over the centuries, people from many different cultures settled in this area, so most Sindhis are actually a mixture of ethnic groups, including Persian, Turkish and Arab.

Left: These elderly men are spending some leisure time in the breathtaking countryside of northern Punjab province. Elderly people in Pakistan are usually treated with great respect.

Most Pashtuns live in North-West Frontier province, but some live in the northern part of Balochistan province. Their **ancestors** were ancient Aryans.

The ancestors of the Baloch people are from Syria. They came to the area that is now Balochistan over fourteen centuries ago. The Baloch lifestyle is growing crops and raising animals.

Muhajirs are Muslims from India. They settled in Pakistan around the time it became a separate nation. Most muhajirs live in Pakistan's large cities.

Left: Members of Pakistani families depend on each other and spend a lot of time together. This large family in the city of Lahore is taking a ride together in a horse-drawn carriage.

Family Life

Pakistani families are often large and many generations of relatives may live together in the same household. The oldest male family member is the head of the household. Traditionally, men work to support the family, while women run the household and raise the children.

City and Countryside

In the cities of Pakistan, rich people live in large, modern houses, but most city dwellers live in small, old houses in crowded neighbourhoods. Large cities are so crowded that almost one-fourth of the people live in **shanty towns**.

Houses in countryside villages are usually made of mud bricks and straw. Some houses in the villages do not even have electricity or running water. The living conditions in many parts of Pakistan cause serious health risks.

Left: This mother and her children live in North-West Frontier province. Like so many of Pakistan's people, they face health problems because of poor sewage disposal and a shortage of safe drinking water.

Education

The education system in Pakistan has five levels. Elementary school is for children between the ages of five and ten. Middle school, for children aged ten to thirteen, is followed by two years of high school. After high school, some students attend an intermediate college, or higher secondary school, for two more years. To attend a university, a student must pass an examination at the end of the second year of college.

Below: Both boys and girls attend this elementary school, but in most parts of the country, boys and girls attend separate schools. Traditionally, in Pakistan, educating boys is considered more important than educating girls.

Literacy and Other Problems

Fewer than half of the Pakistani people over the age of fifteen can read and write. The **literacy** rate is lower among the people who live in the countryside because they have fewer opportunities for education. Pakistan does not have enough schools, especially in rural areas, and the schools the country does have do not have enough trained teachers and classroom materials.

Above: Many rural schools do not have enough classrooms. This schoolteacher from Balochistan province is giving a lesson to some elementary school children outdoors.

Religion

Islam is Pakistan's official religion. About 97 per cent of the country's population are Muslims from one of two main groups. Sunni Muslims are the largest Islamic group. About three-quarters of the country's Muslims are Sunni. The other main group is Shi'a Muslims. Only about 3 per cent of the people in Pakistan are not Muslims. Most of them are Hindus or Christians. Others are Sikhs, Parsis or Ahmadis.

Below: Badshahi Mosque is one of the places Muslims in Lahore go to pray. This huge, red sandstone structure was built in the late 1600s by Mughal emperor Aurangzeb.

The Islamic Faith

All Muslims believe in one God, called Allah, and His prophet or messenger, named Muhammad. In practising their faith, Muslims are supposed to pray to Allah five times a day. They are also expected to give money to the poor. Each year during the holy month of Ramadan, Muslims do not eat or drink anything during the day. Every Muslim also tries to visit the holy city of Mecca at least once in his or her lifetime.

Above: The city of Lahore has a small number of people who belong to the Sikh religion. This building is a Sikh temple.

Language

With so many ethnic groups, Pakistan also has many languages, but only two, Urdu and English, are the country's official languages. Urdu is much like Hindi, the language of India, except it uses many Persian and Arabic words, and it is written from right to left. Not very many Pakistanis speak English, but it is widely used in government, business and higher education.

Left: Most of the newspapers and magazines that are published in Pakistan are in Urdu, English or one of a few other languages. Many Pakistanis speak their own ethnic languages, which include Balochi, Brahui, Punjabi, Pashtu and Sindhi.

Left:
These Muslim boys attend a religious school in Karachi. They are reading the Qur'an, which is the holy book of the Islamic faith.

Literature

Since the sixteenth century, most of Pakistan's literature has been written in Urdu. Faiz Ahmad Faiz (1911–1984) is a well-known Urdu poet. Saadat Hasan Manto (1912–1955) is known for his short stories. Ahmad Nadeem Qasimi (1916–) writes about life in the countryside. Sir Muhammad Iqbl (1877–1938) is considered Pakistan's most famous poet. Although he lived before Pakistan became a nation, he was the first to propose forming an independent state for Muslims.

Arts

During the time of the Mughal Empire, painting was an important art form. The styles developed by Mughal painters are still reflected in Pakistani art today. The works of Pakistan's leading painter, Abdur Rahman Chughtai (1897–1975), are done in traditional Mughal style.

Modern art came to Pakistan in the 1950s. Pakistani artists of the twentieth century such as Shakir Ali (1916–1975) and Zubeida Agha (1922–1997) used Western painting techniques.

Left: Sadequain (1930–1987) is one of Pakistan's most popular modern artists. Here are two of his figure paintings. His other works include **murals** and calligraphy.

Left: This painting, titled *Blue Vase*, is one of Zubeida Agha's creations. Agha completed *Blue Vase* in 1993, four years before he died.

Below: Decorated trucks like this one are a modern art form in Pakistan.

Art on Wheels

Trucks and buses painted with brightly coloured designs are popular throughout Pakistan. The designs can be anything from flowers and landscapes to animals and aeroplanes. The designs on some vehicles include verses from the Qur'an.

Left: Some of the art that decorates Pakistan's mosques and other buildings are paintings that include calligraphy. Even objects such as plates and vases are often decorated with calligraphy.

Calligraphy and Handicrafts

The art of beautiful handwriting, which is called calligraphy, has been popular in Pakistan for hundreds of years. The calligraphy artists of Pakistan usually write out poems or verses from the Qur'an. Some also use calligraphy to make border patterns in books.

Every province in Pakistan has its own handicrafts. Punjab potters make clay toys that look like objects from the ancient Indus Valley civilisation.

Sindh province is also known for its pottery, embroidery and a craft known as mirrorwork, which is sewing tiny pieces of mirror onto cloth.

Folk Dancing

With so many ethnic groups, Pakistan has many different folk dances. In the Punjabi dance *bhangra*, men sing and dance in a circle around a drummer. The dance starts slowly, then gets faster and faster. *Khattak* is a Pashtun sword dance.

Left: These men are performing a traditional Sindhi folk dance. Many of Pakistan's folk dances are very lively. Some are often performed only by men.

Leisure

Most of Pakistan's leisure activities are the kinds that bring friends and families together. After Friday prayers, Muslims often stay at the mosque to share news with friends. Hobbies and weekly trips to the market are some other activities that bring people together. Men in rural areas like to get together at cockfights and pigeon or camel races. Cities offer a greater variety of entertainment.

Above: Pakistanis love to watch movies, which are available in all cities and even in many villages.

Left: In Pakistan's cities, public parks are popular places for family activities, such as picnics and camel rides. Some cities also have amusement parks.

Left: The children in Pakistan like to play board games. These boys are playing a game called ludo, which is a favourite board game in both India and Pakistan.

Television and Games

Most families in Pakistan have TV sets. The programmes they watch include news reports, quiz shows, soap operas and reruns of old comedies from western countries. Wealthier families with video recorders are able to watch new programmes from the West on videotapes.

Pakistani children play their own versions of games such as marbles, tag and hide-and-seek, which are familiar to children all over the world. They also enjoy flying kites.

Cricket

The British introduced cricket to British India in the 1700s. Today, Pakistanis play cricket locally, nationally and internationally, and some of the world's best players, such as Imran Khan, Wasim Akram and Mushtaq Ahmed, are from Pakistan. Cricket is played with a bat and a ball and two teams, each with eleven players. The rules for cricket are fairly complicated.

Below: Field hockey is a very popular sport in Pakistan. The country's national team has won three Olympic gold medals and four World Cup championships.

Left: At the age of seventeen, Jahangir Khan (*left*) became the youngest winner of the World Open Championship in squash. He was also the winner of the British Open Championship ten times in a row.

Other Sports

Hockey, squash and polo are just a few of the other sports played in Pakistan. Polo is a team sport that is played on horseback. Players try to score points by hitting a ball with a stick, called a mallet, into the other team's goal. Pakistan has played a dominant role in the game of squash for many years. The Khan family has won more than 80 per cent of tournament titles. Jahangir Khan is just one member of the Khan family who has dominated the game.

Muslim Holy Days

For one month each year, all healthy, adult Muslims must fast, which means they do not eat or drink during daylight hours. This time of fasting celebrates Ramadan, the holiest month in the Muslim calendar. Eid ul-Fitr is a festival that marks the end of Ramadan. ***Bakr-Id***, or Feast of the **Sacrifice**, is celebrated at the end of the Islamic year.

Above: Muslims celebrate the end of Ramadan with prayers and feasts. These Muslims are praying at Badshahi Mosque, in Lahore, on the morning of Eid ul-Fitr.

Other Holidays

Besides religious holy days, Pakistan also has national holidays. Independence Day is on 14 August. On this day, homes and businesses display the flag to celebrate India's break with Britain, which made Pakistan a separate nation. On 6 September, Defence of Pakistan Day, military parades held throughout the country remember the **conflict** between Pakistan and India in 1965.

Below: Islamabad celebrates Pakistan Day on 23 March with a parade and fireworks. This holiday honours the 1940 resolution by which Muslims demanded an independent state.

Food

Bread, rice and vegetables are the most common foods eaten daily in Pakistan. Pakistanis also eat meat and poultry when they can afford to buy it.

Pakistanis often eat a bread called chapati. It is round and flat, like a tortilla, but when it is heated, chapati becomes soft and puffy. Chapati fried in butter is a popular bread called paratha.

Left: Pakistani cooking uses a lot of herbs and spices, including red and green chillies, garlic and ginger. Yoghurt is an ingredient in many recipes because it helps make the taste of hot spices milder.

Left: Each province in Pakistan has its own special dishes. Punjab province is known for its bread and different kinds of dal, while Sindh province specialises in seafood dishes.

Besides eating plain white rice, many Pakistanis enjoy biryani, which is rice that has been cooked in a meat sauce.

Favourite vegetable dishes include dal, which is lentils, beans or peas spiced with garlic, onions, chillies, cloves, ginger and black pepper.

Tea, usually with milk and lots of sugar added, is Pakistan's most popular drink. Lassi, which is a combination of yoghurt and mango juice, is another favourite Pakistani beverage.

PAKISTAN

Above: This man is making sweets to sell at a market in Peshawar.

Afghanistan A3–D1
Arabian Sea A4–C5

Balochistan
   (province) A4–C3
Balochistan
   Plateau A3–A4

China D1

Federally
   Administered
   Tribal Areas C2

Himalayas C1–D2
Hindu Kush
   Range C1

India C5–D2
Indus Plain B4–C3
Indus River B5–D2
Indus Valley C3–C4
Iran A1–A4
Islamabad C2
Islamabad Capital
   Territory C2

K2 D1
Karachi B4
Karakoram
   Range D1

Lahore D3

Mohenjo-Daro B4

Northern Areas
   C1–D2
North-West Frontier
   (province) C1–C3

Peshawar C2
Punjab (province)
   C3–D2

Sindh (province)
   B3–C5

Tajikistan B1–D1
Turkmenistan
   A1–B1

Uzbekistan B1

Quick Facts

Official Name	Islamic Republic of Pakistan
Capital	Islamabad
Official Languages	Urdu, English
Population	159,196,336 (July 2004 estimate)
Land Area	803,940 square kilometres
Administrative Regions	Balochistan, Federally Administered Tribal Areas, Islamabad Capital Territory, North-West Frontier, Punjab, Sindh
Highest Point	K2 (8,611 metres)
Main River	Indus
Main Religion	Islam
National Holidays	Pakistan Day (23 March)
	Independence Day (14 August)
	Defence of Pakistan Day (6 September)
	Birth and death anniversaries of Muhammad Ali Jinnah (25 December and 11 September)
Religious Festivals	Ramadan, Bakr-Id, Eid ul-Fitr
Currency	Pakistani rupees (108.198 PKR = £1 as of 2004)

Opposite: This man is wearing a round, flat wool cap called a Hunza hat. It is part of the traditional clothing worn by the Pashtun people, who live in North-West Frontier province.

Glossary

alpine: related to areas of land at very high elevations, especially mountain slopes above the timberline.

ancestors: family members from past generations.

Aryans: a people who settled in the regions of Iran and northern India around 1500 B.C.

Bakr-Id: a Muslim holy day or festival honouring the faith of Abraham, who, according to the Bible, was willing to sacrifice his only son to show his belief in God.

civilisation: a highly developed society with an established government and culture and a written history.

conflict: a fight, struggle or clash due to opposing views or interests.

corruption: dishonesty or illegal activity, usually to gain money or power.

coup: a sudden military action to take over a government.

crescent: a thin, curved moon shape.

diverse: having many differences and much variety.

ethnic: related to a group of people from a particular country or culture.

federal republic: a nation in which the citizens elect representatives to run the central government.

fertile: able to support growth or produce offspring.

flourished: grew or developed quickly and successfully.

humid: damp, usually describing the amount of moisture in the air.

literacy: the ability to read and write.

murals: large pictures painted directly on walls or ceilings.

parliament: an official government body of elected representatives who make the laws of their country.

plateau: a wide area of high, flat land.

sacrifice: the act of giving up personal needs or wants so that others will have what they need or want.

shanty towns: sections of cities where people live in crudely-built shelters.

Sikh: belonging to a religion of India known as Sikhism, which combines Hindu and Islamic beliefs.

threshing: separating the grains or seeds of a cereal plant, such as wheat.

More Books to Read

Conflict: India and Pakistan. David Downing (Heinemann Library)

Country File, Pakistan. Ian Graham (Franklin Watts)

Indus Valley City. Gillian Clements (Franklin Watts)

Pakistan. Letters from Around the World series. David Cumming
   (Evans Publishing Group)

Pakistan. World Focus series. Elspeth Clayton (Heinemann Library)

Web Sites

www.ancientindia.co.uk/indus/home_set.html

www.harappa.com

www.islamabad.com

www.punjab-info.fsnet.co.uk/lahore.html

Due to the dynamic nature of the Internet, some web sites stay current longer than others. To find additional web sites, use a reliable search engine with one or more of the following keywords to help you locate information about Pakistan. Keywords: *Ali Jinnah, Balochistan, Bhutto, Indus River, Islamabad, Lahore, Mohenjo-Daro.*

Note to parents and teachers
Every effort has been made by the Publishers to ensure that these web sites are suitable for children; that they are of the highest educational value, and that they contain no inappropriate or offensive material. However, because of the nature of the Internet, it is impossible to guarantee that the contents of these sites will not be altered. We strongly advise that Internet access is supervised by a responsible adult.

Index